Canada Recycles

Peter Cook and Laura Suzuki

Scholastic Canada Ltd.
Toronto New York London Auckland Sydney
Mexico City New Delhi Hong Kong Buenos Aires

Scholastic Canada Ltd.
604 King Street West, Toronto, Ontario M5V 1E1, Canada

Scholastic Inc.
557 Broadway, New York, NY 10012, USA

Scholastic Australia Pty Limited
PO Box 579, Gosford, NSW 2250, Australia

Scholastic New Zealand Limited
Private Bag 94407, Botany, Manukau 2163, New Zealand

Scholastic Children's Books
Euston House, 24 Eversholt Street, London NW1 1DB, UK

Library and Archives Canada Cataloguing in Publication

Cook, Peter, 1965-
Canada recycles / Peter Cook and Laura Suzuki.

(Canada close up)
Includes index.
ISBN 978-1-4431-0715-0

1. Recycling (Waste, etc.)--Canada--Juvenile literature.
2. Waste minimization--Canada--Juvenile literature.
3. Refuse and refuse disposal--Canada--Juvenile literature.
I. Suzuki, Laura, 1964- II. Title. III. Series: Canada close up (Toronto, Ont.)

TD794.5.C66 2012   j363.72'820971   C2011-905476-0

6 5 4 3 2 1   Printed in Canada   119   12 13 14 15 16 17

The pages of this book are printed on paper that contains 100% post-consumer waste.

Table of Contents

Pronunciation Guide

a as in c**a**t; **ah** as in c**a**ll; **ay** as in pl**a**te; **ee** as in s**ee**; **eh** as in p**e**t; **eye** as in cr**y**; **i** as in p**i**t; **oh** as in **o**cean; **oo** as in f**oo**d; **ur** as in f**ur**; **uh** as in b**u**t

Chapter 1

Dealing with Waste

Early humans didn't make much garbage. When they did leave waste — flesh, bone, wood, stone — it was natural, from plants, animals or minerals.

Over the years as people invented better tools, more waste was produced. As blacksmiths began to shape metal by forging it, they learned that they could melt their scrap metal to use it again. People didn't throw out much because man-made goods were rare and expensive.

Fast-forward to today. People have gotten used to throwing things away. More and more items are made to be **disposable**. This is becoming a big problem because the number of people on Earth is growing.

We buy a lot of stuff, and nothing we use lasts forever. In time everything becomes garbage, and we have to figure out how to get rid of it.

Son of War Eagle Landfill, Whitehorse, Yukon

What to do with garbage seems simple: just throw it in a trash bag and take it to the dump, or wait for the garbage truck to come by. What could be easier than that?

But what happens to all those bags of garbage? Is throwing all that stuff out the only thing we can do?

At some point, we have to start changing how we deal with garbage. It would be best not to throw anything away. But that is not possible yet. So we have to start taking responsibility for the waste we make.

To cut down on our garbage we can follow the three Rs:

- Reduce: Use less stuff so new **products** don't have to be made in the first place.
- Reuse: Use things over again rather than throwing them away and buying new items.
- Recycle: Make new things out of old items.

Chapter 2

Why Recycle?

Why recycle at all? Why not just dump everything and make new stuff?

We can't always make new products. We are running out of the supplies, or **natural resources**, we make them from.

We get our wood and paper from trees. But most of the world's forests have been cut or burned down. Metals are used to make everything from cars to coins to electronics. But it's getting harder to find places to mine metals. Also, collecting these resources causes a lot of harm to the environment and to animal and plant habitats.

Then there is oil. Most of Canada's energy comes from oil and natural gas, which are getting harder to find. We are using them up. Our use of oil also causes harm to the environment, especially in the form of **climate change**. Since most plastics are made from oil, recycling plastic can help reduce our use of it.

Prairie pumpjacks bring oil to the surface

We also need to recycle because garbage has to go somewhere. A large city has enough people to produce millions of tonnes of garbage every year. It's a big problem to figure out where to dump all that trash. Most garbage goes to **landfill sites** — large pieces of land where our waste is buried.

What's the difference between a garbage dump and a landfill site? People used to find a place nearby to "dump" their garbage. They kept dumping there until it filled up. Now we choose these sites carefully. Landfills are not put near water sources. They are built with liners to keep anything poisonous from leaking into the ground underneath.

As garbage is brought in, a landfill site slowly fills up. Then a new site has to be found. That's getting harder to do. Even though we have plenty of empty space in Canada, not much of it is near our big cities. So garbage has to be taken farther away. This costs more and uses more energy.

New landfill sites also cost a lot because they must be made safe. Many old landfills and dumps leak **methane**, a dangerous **greenhouse gas**, into the air. It is expensive to keep an eye on these dirty old dumps and clean them up.

Crane Mountain Landfill in New Brunswick has several lined landfill cells. When one fills up, it is capped and a new one is opened.

The Crane Mountain Landfill collects the gas created by the waste. The gas powers the generator (machinery on the right side). This creates enough energy to run the site and two hundred homes.

New Brunswick is the leader in landfill management. In 1998, it closed all of its old dumps — over three hundred of them — and created six regional landfills. The landfills have special thick liners to keep in anything that could leak out into the soil. Any leaks are cleaned, and the water is taken out. The methane gas is burned off. Recently New Brunswick has been building power plants that use the burning methane to make electricity.

Chapter 3

From the Bin to the Plant

In Canada, the provinces make their own rules about waste management and recycling. It is up to each city or town to follow the rules in its own way.

There are two systems for recycling. One is the depot (DEE-poh) system, where people bring their recyclables to one location. The other system is curbside pickup, where recyclables are put out in collection boxes and are taken away to the **recycling plant**.

A recycling depot in Edmonton

A depot system means that you have to bring your items to a depot station and you sort them into bins. In this way the recyclables are sorted before they go to separate plants to be recycled. This is faster and easier for the recyclers. The depot could be the store you bought the item from, but in many cases it's a separate location.

With curbside pickup, each household puts all of its recycling into one or two bins. Once the recycling has been collected by the collection trucks, it needs to be separated by type at the recycling plant.

Since throwing all of your recycling into a blue box is easy, it encourages more people to recycle. But with everything mixed together, it makes it harder and more expensive to sort at the plant. The blue-box system also doesn't work well for apartment buildings, which are often built with just a garbage chute.

Canada's first "blue box" curbside pickup program started in Kitchener, Ontario, in 1981. The colour blue was chosen because it stood out and was least likely to fade in strong sunlight.

In the depot system, the items to be returned may have deposits on them — you pay a few cents more at the store for your pop, and get the money back when you return the bottle. The best known example of this in Canada is the beer bottle deposit. Bottles can be returned for cash.

In some provinces, wine bottles and other drink containers can also be taken back to the store or a depot. In Newfoundland and Labrador, bottle depots take all kinds of drink containers and return the deposits. In British Columbia, school clubs and other groups are known for their bottle drives, which raise money by collecting bottles for the deposits.

The depot system works best when depots accept all types of recyclables at each location, or if the depots are in the stores where the items were bought. When depots for different items are far apart, people are less likely to recycle.

Used paint and televisions at Gibsons Recycling Depot in British Columbia

British Columbia is the Canadian leader in creating depot systems — it has (or is planning) depots for antifreeze, batteries, cell phones, electronics, smoke alarms, paint, small appliances, oil and other items.

Most large cities and towns have curbside pickup. In some places, people sort paper and other recyclables into separate containers. Collection trucks keep the different recyclables apart. This makes sorting at the recycling plant easier, cheaper and more complete.

In other places everything is put in the same container and taken to the recycling plant. This is easier for people — everything gets thrown into one bin, no thinking needed. But it is more work (and it costs more) for the recycling plant to have to sort everything into separate types.

In either case, after the recycling has been collected it goes to a recycling plant. The different types of recyclables will be further sorted there. Then they can be sent to processing plants to be turned into something new.

At the recycling plant, everything is dumped into a huge pile. The pile is then shovelled onto a moving conveyor belt by large front-end loaders. For easy sorting the pile is spread out with a big roller. Any large items are stopped and checked over.

Unrecyclable things — like car parts and construction tools — are removed from the belt. These kinds of things should never be put in household recycling.

Also at this point any plastic bags or plastic sheets are often removed, as they could get caught in the machinery.

Chapter 4

Recycling Paper

Depending on their machinery, different recycling plants sort out recyclables in different orders. Some plants sort out glass early in the process. Others do it near the end.

Big, flat items like cardboard boxes or paper usually lie on top of other recycling. They're often removed first using **mechanical sorting**. The first sorter has a set of large discs that spin. These discs are sized and spaced so that large, flat pieces of cardboard slide over them. The cardboard is sent on a belt to be checked and **baled**. The rest of the material falls through the spaces between the discs and lands on another moving belt.

Cardboard is being sorted by revolving disks.

That belt leads to another set of discs that are designed to remove newspaper, magazines and boxboard. Again, the rest of the items fall to the next section of the conveyor belt.

Mixed paper — envelopes, letter paper, notepaper and other light scraps — is then passed through another screen and blown by air onto another conveyor belt. The paper is checked over and sent to a large pile for bundling.

Paper can be made from many different materials, such as linen or cotton. But most paper these days is made from **wood pulp**, which comes from trees. When paper is recycled, fewer trees have to be cut down to produce paper.

At the processing plant, the collected paper is turned back into pulp by soaking it. While white paper from offices can be recycled as clean white paper, household paper has to be cleaned and de-inked. This is done by adding soaps and other foaming chemicals to the pulpy mess. Ink and other gunk, like glue and dirt, stick to the foam and get rinsed away.

Corrugated cardboard, which is often used to make boxes, is recycled to become new corrugated cardboard. Newsprint is used for more newsprint. Mixed paper is used for different paper products. Sometimes new paper pulp is added to the recycled pulp to make it stronger or a better quality.

Both new and recycled white paper get their bright colour by using bleach or hydrogen peroxide. Since chlorine bleach is poisonous to the environment, look for non-chlorine-bleached paper products, marked with the letters PCF (Process Chlorine-Free).

Chapter 5

Recycling Glass

Even if a province has a bottle deposit program, glass jars still go into curbside collection. By the time glass makes it to the plant, most of it is broken. It first got bashed around in a truck with your neighbour's recycling, then moved by loaders at the recycling plant. It has probably been run over a few times.

Machines and human line workers sort the glass pieces by colour. Since melted glass keeps its colour, clear glass (the most useful) must be sorted carefully from green and amber.

Glass being crushed into cullet

At the glass processing plant, sorted glass is crushed into tiny pieces called cullet. Then it is ready to be melted to make new glass. Coloured cullet is sometimes ground into a fine powder to use for sandblasting, or to make fibreglass materials.

Not all glass can be used in recycling plants. Window glass, light bulbs, oven-safe glassware and drinking glasses are made from different recipes than bottle glass, so they must stay out of city collection bins. If cullets of different chemical types are mixed together, they will not melt properly. This makes poor-quality glass.

Cullet, sorted by colour, at a bottle-making factory

Chapter 6

Recycling Metals

Different metals have been used since the beginning of human history. All metals can be melted down and reused forever, so they are perfect for recycling. Most of the metal from household recycling comes from drink and food cans, which are made of either steel or aluminum.

At the recycling plant, metals are sorted with magnets. Steel is attracted to the magnets, so it gets pulled up to a magnetic conveyor belt that passes over the main belt. Aluminum isn't magnetic, so it doesn't get attracted to that belt.

Steel cans being pulled up from the conveyor by magnets

But there are certain ways magnets can affect metals that are not magnetic. As the aluminum cans move along, a moving magnetic field kicks them across a dip in the belt into a separate chute.

This magnetic field is called an eddy current. It is like the push-back you get when you try to put two of the same magnet poles together.

Aluminum cans being pushed around by an eddy current

The sorted metal cans are crushed flat and stacked in bales, ready to be sent to a **foundry.** There the cans are melted down into sheets or blocks and will be used to make new metal items.

Bronze and copper are valuable metals, and metal foundries will pay a lot for them. Thieves often steal valuable copper plumbing pipes from construction sites. Even bronze statues have been stolen to be melted down for their recycling value. This is a form of recycling that shouldn't be done!

Chapter 7

Recycling Plastics

At a recycling plant, plastic containers are scanned and sorted by their type and removed from the conveyor belt.

In newer plants this is mainly done by **optical scanners**. They use special light beams to pick out what type of plastic each object is. The different plastics get sorted into different bins by jets of air controlled by the machine. Older recycling plants use optical scanners and human sorters to scan the fast-moving belt, identify the plastic types and then sort them into separate bins.

An optical scanner (the light seen here) picks out different types of plastics

There are many kinds of plastics, and they need to be recycled in different ways. Plastic items are numbered from 1 to 7. Each number tells you the type of plastic the product is made of.

Type 1 is polyethylene terephthalate (paw-lee-EH-thi-leen tehr-af-THA-late), or PETE. This is used to make pop and water bottles, peanut butter jars, fruit, vegetable and cake trays and polyester fibres. Type 1 plastics are the most easily recycled. Piles of this plastic are crushed into bales to be sold to processing companies.

At the processing plant, clear type 1 may be separated from coloured type 1. It's more valuable, since it can be used for a lot more things. The bales are cleaned of food bits, paper labels and caps, then shredded into tiny flakes. The flakes are melted down and reused to make new products.

Type 2 is high-density polyethylene, or HDPE. This is used to make bottles for milk, juice, bleach and shampoo, as well as yogurt tubs. Type 2 plastic flakes can be recycled to make blue boxes, drainage tubes and even plastic lumber. Type 2 can also be combined with types 4 and 5 to make laundry hampers, baskets, storage containers and shelves.

Pellets made from recycled plastic can be melted to make new things.

Type 3 is polyvinyl chloride (paw-lee-VEYE-nel CLOR-eyed), or PVC, and vinyl. This plastic is used to make construction pipes and fittings, "clamshell" containers for food, medical tubing and cables. PVC is often used in construction because it is very cheap to make, and it will last for years. It's not used much in households, so it isn't usually part of city recycling programs.

Type 4 is low-density polyethylene, or LDPE. This is used in bread bags, squeezable bottles and toys. Type 4 makes good packaging — it's tough and can be easy to see through. It can be recycled to make floor tiles, furniture, trash cans and outdoor lumber.

Toys made from recycled plastics

Type 5 is polypropylene (paw-lee-PRO-pi-leen), or PP. This is used in medicine bottles, some unrecyclable packaging and ice cream tubs. It can be recycled to make battery cables for cars, bicycle racks, ice scrapers and storage bins.

Recyclable mixing bowls made from recycled type 5 plastic

Type 6 is polystyrene (paw-lee-STEYE-reen), or PS. It is used in CD jewel cases, meat trays, foam egg trays and takeout cups, Styrofoam peanuts and snap-off yogurt cups. Polystyrene can be recycled to make items like picture frames.

Type 7 is any other plastics and mixed-filler plastics that don't fit into the other six types. It can be recycled as filler plastic.

It is important to make sure that any plastics sent for household recycling haven't held poisonous chemicals. This is why it's difficult to recycle used plastic into new containers for food. One bottle used to store gasoline or weed killer can make a whole batch of recycled plastic unusable for food storage.

Juice boxes and other drink cartons, such as Tetra Paks, are made of layers of paper, aluminum and plastic. They are sorted with plastics. Bales of these boxes are shipped to special factories, where they're cut into tiny pieces and made into plastic pellets. These pellets still contain the pieces of paper and aluminum, as it is hard to separate the layers. They are used in making plastic flower containers and some construction materials.

Any scraps left on a conveyor belt — tiny bits of glass, paper and plastic — are thrown away as garbage because there's no easy way to deal with them.

Not every city in Canada recycles every type of plastic. But there are recycling companies that do use the materials, and new ways to recycle them are always being found.

You can be creative and find your own way to recycle things at home – like these reusable gift boxes made from juice cartons!

Chapter 8

Beyond the Recycling Plant

There are lots of other things that can be recycled, but it costs more money and takes more work. Some provinces have started recycling programs for these items.

Electronic items make up a lot of household waste — all the MP3 players, televisions, computers and phones that we throw out when we buy new ones.

Electronics are made of materials that can be recycled, such as glass, plastics and metals. But they also contain other stuff that isn't recyclable. Some of it — including poisonous chemicals — is dangerous.

Parts of broken computers can be removed and reused. There are companies that take old computers apart to use the pieces that still work, like hard drives.

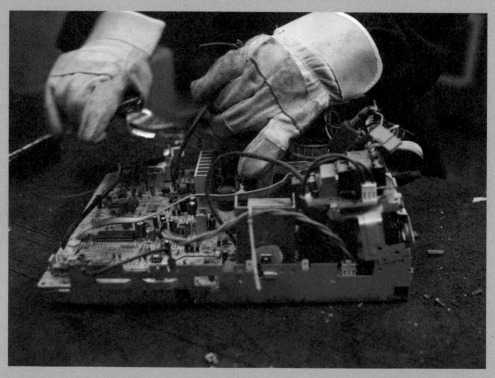

A worker carefully takes an old television apart so its pieces can be recycled.

At the recycling centre, an electronic item is taken apart by hand. The pieces are separated into different types, such as metals, plastics, circuit boards, leaded glass, batteries and parts containing mercury. These get sent for more processing at different plants. The pieces that can't be used are sent to landfill or toxic-waste disposals.

Recycling electronics is expensive to do. Strict safety measures must be taken to protect workers because of the toxic chemicals. But, to save money, some companies ship electronics to be recycled in countries with very few health and safety laws for their workers.

The best thing to do with electronics that still work is to see if they can be sold or given away. Maybe a friend, younger sister or brother or grandparent would like to try an MP3 player. Perhaps a local charity needs a computer. It may not be the newest and best, but it will still work just fine.

Tires are another thing we throw away in huge numbers. Every car or truck needs tires in good condition to drive safely. Once tire treads wear down, it becomes much harder for a vehicle to stop, especially in rain or snow. Every few years, tire treads wear out and all the tires have to be replaced with a new set.

But what do you do with all these old tires? It's important to keep them out of garbage dumps because they're large and take up a lot of space. Because tires are made out of oil products, if a tire dump catches fire it can burn for a long time.

In 1990, a tire dump in Hagersville, Ontario, caught fire and burned for seventeen days, polluting the area and exposing firefighters to toxic chemicals.

If a truck tire is in good shape, it can have new treads put on. Old treads are ground off and new treads are stuck on through a difficult process. Then it is sold as a retread. Tires can be retreaded many times, stretching their lifespan by years.

Tires that aren't retreaded are ground up into tiny pieces called crumb rubber. Crumb rubber can be used to make things like rubber playground surfaces, mats and athletic tracks. It can be added to asphalt to pave roads. Even better, tire makers are working with recyclers to add some crumb rubber to the recipe for new tires. They're trying to figure out new ways to use more of the rubber from old tires.

Clothing is something else we make and throw away. It's easy to end up with piles of good clothes that can't be worn anymore. Kids grow out of their pants. Adults gain or lose weight and need new clothes. Styles change.

Clothes that are in good shape are often reused, not recycled. They can be passed down to family or friends. Baby clothes often get passed through several families, since babies usually grow out of clothes before the items wear out.

Expensive and fashionable clothing with little wear can be taken to consignment shops, which sell the clothes and give some of the money to the original owner. Other clothing can be taken to thrift stores, where they are sold to raise money for charity.

What about the organic waste from your food and yard? One of the best (and easiest) ways to get rid of things like grass clippings and apple peels is to start a composter or compost heap in your backyard. When things rot, or decay, tiny organisms, like bacteria, fungi and insects, eat and digest them. This breaks the organic waste down into humus (HYOO-muhs), a rich soil that's perfect for the garden!

Composting is easy. Kitchen scraps are thrown into a large pile or box, along with layers of leaves and grass clippings from the yard. It is important to have both food scraps and leaves in compost, because that will cause things to decay faster. Every few weeks, the compost pile should be stirred to mix in air. This also helps the waste break down faster.

The one problem with composting food is that you can't put in fats or meats. They will attract animal pests. Instead, you could use a digester, which is a container sunk into the ground. This keeps it safe from animals. There, bacteria that don't need oxygen will turn food waste into a liquid that soaks into the soil.

Chapter 9

Living the Three Rs

Recycling is not the answer to everything. Keep in mind that recycling is last on the list of the three Rs. It is not nearly as important as reducing and reusing.

The main problem with recycling is how much it costs. Recyclables take a lot of work to collect, move, store, sort and process. The machinery needed can be very expensive. Recycling companies sell the recycled materials for money. Not many companies want to use recycled material if it costs more than making something from scratch.

People are always thinking of ways to make the recycling system better. For example, researchers are trying to find ways to separate chemicals from plastics as they are melted down. This would keep them from polluting the recycling system.

This kind of research costs money, but it's worth doing. In the future, it may be cheaper to recycle than to create new products.

One of the best ways to improve how we deal with waste is to make little changes in the way we live. Then some of those little changes can gradually get bigger.

The Recycling Council of Ontario has created a program called the Waste-Free Lunch Challenge. For a week, students and teachers try to bring lunches that have nothing in them that can't be eaten (the food), composted (banana peels, apple cores), reused (reusable storage containers) or recycled.

Leftover food, recyclables and garbage are weighed and the amount is totalled over the week. Classes or schools compare the amount of waste left over before and after the challenge. This helps to show how well they've done at protecting the environment by reducing waste.

In your school, why not turn the week into Waste-Free Lunch Month? Spread the word by challenging other classes to do the same, or even the whole school. Some schools have already made waste-free lunches a school-wide policy.

These students from Toronto won the Waste-Free Lunch Challenge in 2010. Part of their prize was to tour an integrated waste-management facility.

The point of doing this is to find ways to reduce garbage every day, and not just during special weeks or months. And not just for lunch, but every meal, and all other times of the day as well.

Here are other ways to make little changes, bit by bit.

- Start an organic garden at home or school. Use compost from your composter to fertilize it.
- Ask your family not to use disposable products like napkins, cups and razors.
- When you shop, think about the packaging. Buy products in packaging that can be easily recycled. Avoid containers that are only used once. Buy in bulk to reduce the amount of packaging.
- Bring your own reusable bag so you don't need to take a plastic shopping bag from the store.
- Refuse junk mail and ask to be removed from mailing lists.

- Repair things rather than buying new ones. If you really need to replace something, consider donating it to charity or holding a yard sale.
- Cut down on takeout dinners.
- Buy secondhand clothes, books, furniture and other items.

Remember:

Don't throw away anything that can be reused or recycled.

Don't buy it unless you really, really need it.

Chapter 10

The Future of the Three Rs

As recycling technologies get better and better, a lot of what we call garbage may soon be okay to recycle. So get used to sorting your trash!

Companies are always looking for new and flashy ways to sell you things. They are still inventing new plastics and mixes of plastics for packaging. This new packaging can't be detected by recycling equipment. Some people will put these new plastics in their recycle bins, even if it's not allowed. And then towns and cities have to figure out how to cover the cost of dealing with this new plastic in the system.

Governments must work with both recycling companies and manufacturers to reduce packaging or make it more recyclable.

We're doing better than we used to. We're now recycling many more things. Some companies pack their goods in smaller or more recyclable packaging. Some stores are insisting on less packaging in the products they sell. Governments are starting to pass laws forcing manufacturers to be part of how their products are finally reused or recycled.

For example, in British Columbia you can return products like light bulbs, batteries, paint, oil and tires to collection depots at stores. Depots, which weren't always easy to get to, are starting to be moved to where people buy the product. Slowly everyone is working towards taking responsibility.

People and companies are always trying
to find the best answers to tricky recycling
questions. For example, which is better:
a glass bottle or a thin plastic package?
A glass bottle can be reused many times,
then recycled — but it takes up storage
space, it costs more to make and is harder
to transport because it weighs a lot. Is a
package made of light, thin plastic better? It
doesn't use much material and is cheap to
transport — but it can't be recycled and will
go straight to the garbage when it's used up.
What do you think?

Recyclers and governments also have to let the makers of recycling equipment know how well their machines work.

The makers often test their machines on clean, dry samples in warm climates, far away from Canadian winters. They need to be told how the scanners and machines actually handle the ice, snow, slush, rain and dirt that our recyclables are often covered with.

And what about the garbage that can't be recycled? Some cities in Europe burn much of their garbage in factories (called **incineration plants**) to make electricity. These waste-to-energy plants have enormous cleaners to keep poisons and pollution out of the air.

But it costs a lot to build such a plant and there are other issues. Will building incinerators change how we treat garbage? Would we make more trash if we thought we could just burn it away?

A waste-to-energy plant in Italy

Would we become more wasteful if we thought it was making more energy? Are we very sure the incinerators are perfectly safe?

These are tough questions. And while there's still lots to do in dealing with garbage, in the past fifty years humans have started to turn themselves around. It's not always easy, and sometimes we will make mistakes. But we can make things better, one step at a time.

Glossary

Baled: Sorted items (plastic bottles, flattened cans [see page 26], etc.) are bound together with cords into box-like bundles.

Climate change: In this book, it refers to changes in Earth's weather patterns that have been caused by humans. When people burn coal or oil they produce greenhouse gases. These gases are added to Earth's atmosphere where they trap heat. This warmer atmosphere can cause huge changes in weather patterns – like storms, droughts and extreme temperatures (hot or cold).

Disposable: A product that is made to be thrown away. Disposable items are usually cheap, often plastic and flimsy rather than durable and long-lasting.

Foundry: A factory that melts metal into liquid in a furnace and then cools the liquid into solid blocks of new metal.

Greenhouse gases: Gases in a planet's atmosphere that absorb heat. When there's too much greenhouse gas, the climate's temperature rises. Common greenhouse gases are carbon dioxide, methane and nitrous oxide.

Incineration plant: A factory which burns garbage as a way to get rid of it. Gases, ash and heat are produced from incineration, and the heat can be used to generate electric power.

Landfill site: A large area where garbage is sent. Garbage dumped in landfills is run over by lots of heavy equipment to flatten it down as much as possible, then covered with soil.

Mechanical sorting: Separating recyclables of different sizes by moving them across screens, spinning wheels or spaces of certain sizes to remove them from a larger group.

Methane: A gas that can be made by the rotting of plant or animal matter in landfills. Methane is also the major part of natural gas, which is used for fuel. It is a greenhouse gas.

Natural resources: Materials occurring in nature, such as minerals, trees or oil, that people use.

Optical scanner: An electronic camera that uses light reflection to sort plastics by type. Different kinds of plastic reflect light in different ways, identifying them for sorting.

Product: Something that is made to be sold.

Recycling plant: 1. A factory for separating recyclables by type (different kinds of paper, metal and plastics) to be used to make new materials. 2. A factory that takes already-sorted material (for example, plastics) and turns it into raw material to make new products.

Wood pulp: Tiny fibres produced when wood is shredded or partially broken down by mechanical and chemical processes. Loads of wood pulp are flattened and dried to make paper.

Index

Acknowledgements

Thanks to the many industry professionals who helped us understand this ever-changing industry: Mary Pickering, Toronto Atmospheric Fund; Robert Gibson, Department of Environmental Studies, University of Waterloo; Maria Kelleher, Kelleher Environmental; Tim Grant, Editor, *Green Teacher* magazine; Dan Lantz, Cascades Recovery Inc. (who put up with many questions, and gave us a tour!); Catherine Leighton, Program Manager – Waste-Free Lunch Challenge, Recycling Council of Ontario; Andrew Horsman, Ontario Tire Stewardship; Robert Cumming, Lafarge North America; Geoff Love, Love Environment Inc.; Jennifer Ellis, Recycling Council of British Columbia; Helen Spiegelman; Janine van Winssen, Fundy Region Solid Waste Commission; Lisa Evangelou, Clean Nova Scotia. Also thanks to Martha Roberts, Alayne Armstrong, Glenn Davies, Paul Mason, Marc Macleod, Tom Simpson and Tamiko Suzuki.

Photo Credits

Cover: Big photo stack © iStockphoto.com/urbancow; Recycling bins © iStockphoto.com/njgphoto; crushed cans © prism68/Shutterstock.com

Interior: p. iv © iStockphoto.com/Michaël Drapeau; p. 2 © Richard Legner/Getty Images; p. 4 © iStockphoto.com/Emily Norton; p. 6 © iStockphoto.com/Stephen Strathdee; p. 8,9 © Fundy Region Solid Waste Commission, photo by Wilson Studio; p. 10 © iStockphoto.com/ Jani Bryson; p. 12 © Kevin Kim, p. 13 © iStockphoto.com/tillsonburg; p. 15 © Gibsons Recycling Depot; p. 17,18,20 © Cascades Recovery Inc.; p. 22 © "© Can Stock Photo Inc./RainerPlendl; p. 24 © iStockphoto.com/Eric Thompson, p. 25 © Sharon McCauley; p. 26 © Huguette Roe/ Shutterstock.com; p. 28,29,30,32 © Cascades Recovery Inc.; p.33 © iStockphoto.com/Miguel Malo; p. 34 © Green Toys Inc.; p. 35 © Preserve, p. 37 © Mary Anne Enriquez, p. 38 © iStockphoto.com/Ermin Gutenberger, p. 40 © iStockphoto.com/Ed Stock, p. 42 © iStockphoto.com/ Ryerson Clark, p. 45 © iStockphoto.com/Martine Doucet, p. 46 © imageegami/Shutterstock.com, p. 50 © Catherine Leighton, p. 51 © iStockphoto.com/ Franky De Meyer, p. 52 © iStockphoto.com/Jani Bryson, p. 55 © Paul Glendell, p. 57 © Drimi /Shutterstock.com.